Money Doesn't Grow on Trees

By
Tony Bland

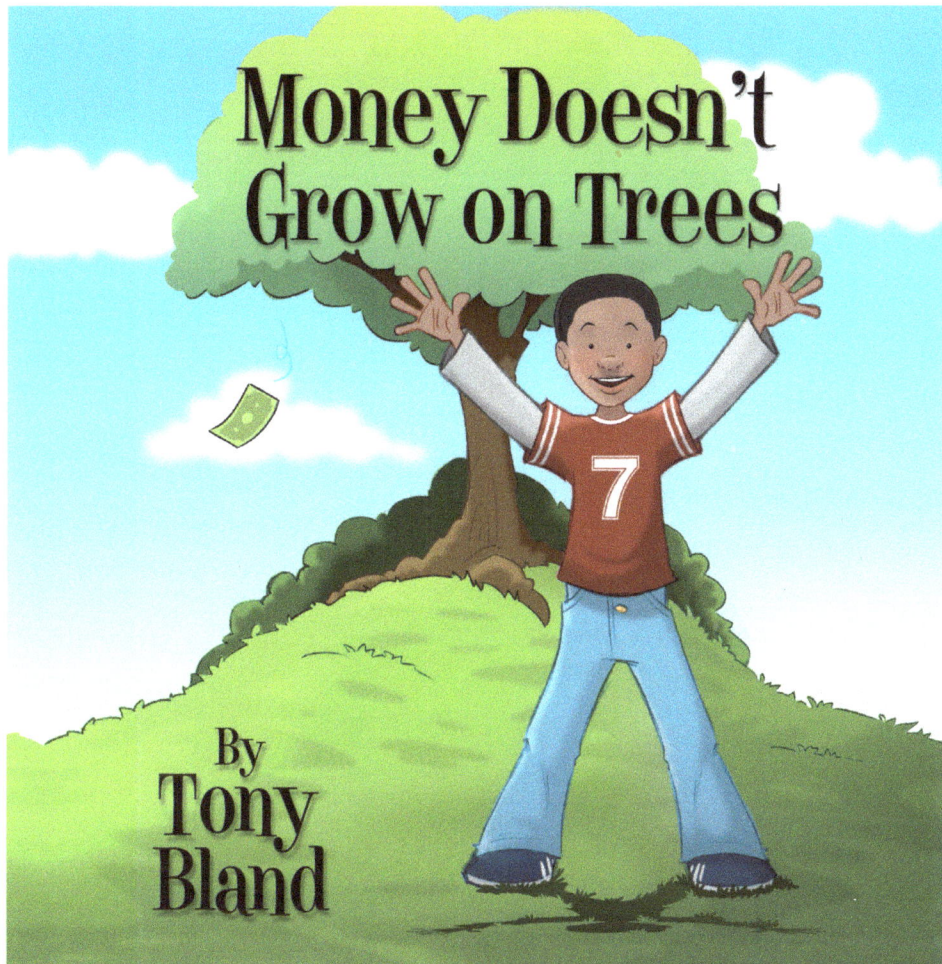

Halo
Publishing International

ISBN 13: 978-1-61244-513-7
Library of Congress Control Number: 2016918243

Printed in the United States of America

Published by Halo Publishing International
1100 NW Loop 410
Suite 700 - 176
San Antonio, Texas 78213
Toll Free 1-877-705-9647
www.halopublishing.com
www.holapublishing.com
e-mail: contact@halopublishing.com

Halo
Publishing International
www.halopublishing.com

I dedicate the book to my hard-working mother, who told me "money doesn't grow on trees" many times throughout my youth, and to my two children, who have been told the same by my wife and me almost as many times.

Born a bright-eyed adventurous child to happy parents and a big sister, Anthony grew quickly into a little boy with lots of energy and big ideas.

5

On a sunny morning in early September, excited for the first day of school, Anthony awoke and over heard his mom telling his older sister, "Money doesn't grow on trees."

Being a curious kid, Anthony thought, "How does money grow?"

After jumping out of bed, eating breakfast, and anxiously heading to school, Anthony thought that his favorite teacher, Ms. Wilson, could probably help him find out all of the ways that money can grow.

Once in class, Anthony thought, "After I find out all the ways that money can grow, I'll set out on an adventure to try to make money grow."

Anthony raised his hand to ask Ms. Wilson a question.

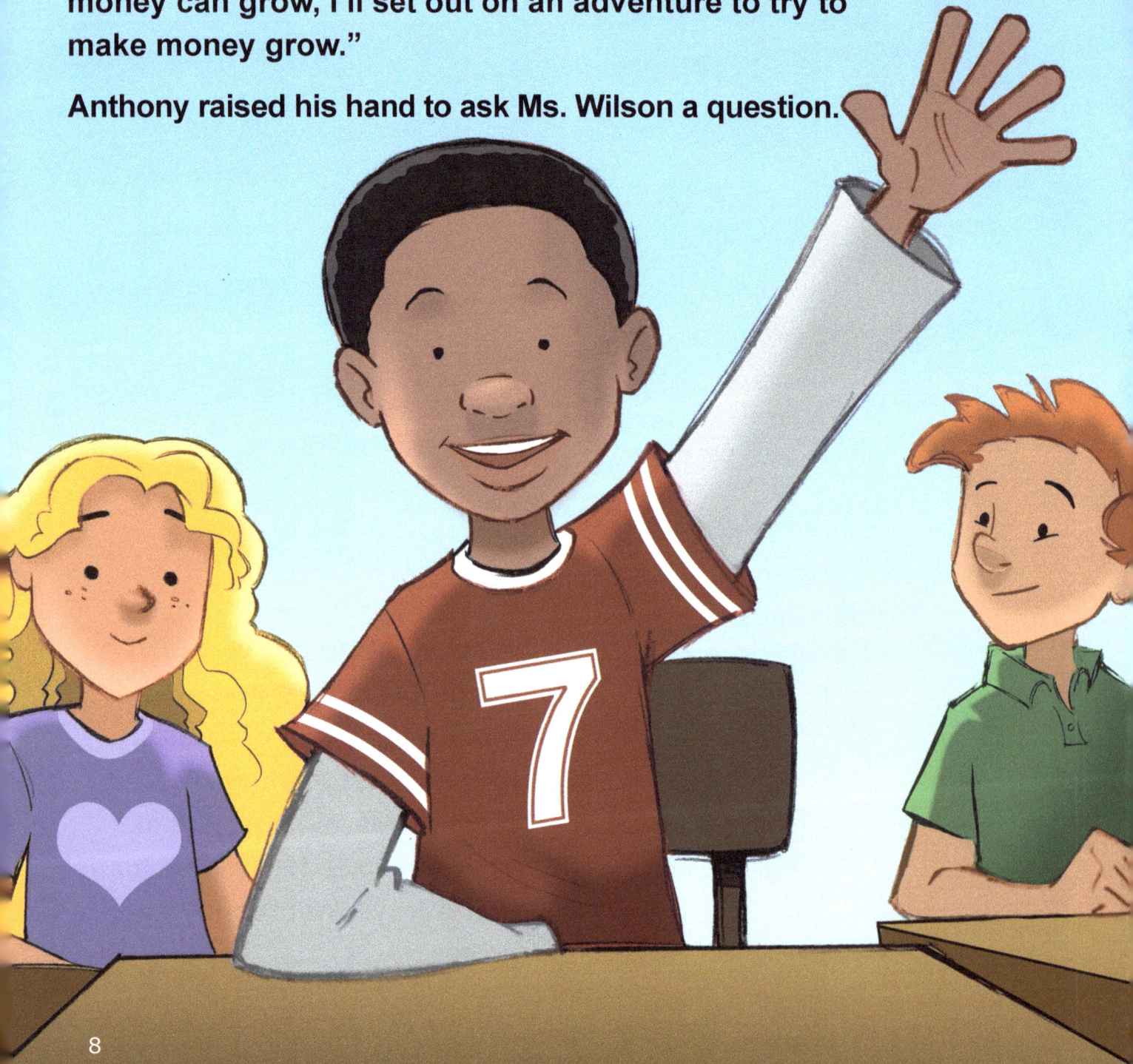

When she called on him, he asked, "Can you help me list all the ways that money can grow?"

A little puzzled by the question, Ms. Wilson said, "Yes, I'll help!"

So, once class ended and all the kids left the classroom, Anthony and Ms. Wilson sat at his desk to make a list.

Ms. Wilson asked Anthony, "How do you think money grows?"

Anthony said aloud, "Hmm, I don't know!"

Ms. Wilson then asked, "Where have you seen money? Maybe that is a good place to start."

Ways To Grow Money

Anthony began to visualize every place he'd seen his parents give people money. Then he began to type the list into his laptop.

Lemonade
$1.00

13

Purchase
tickets

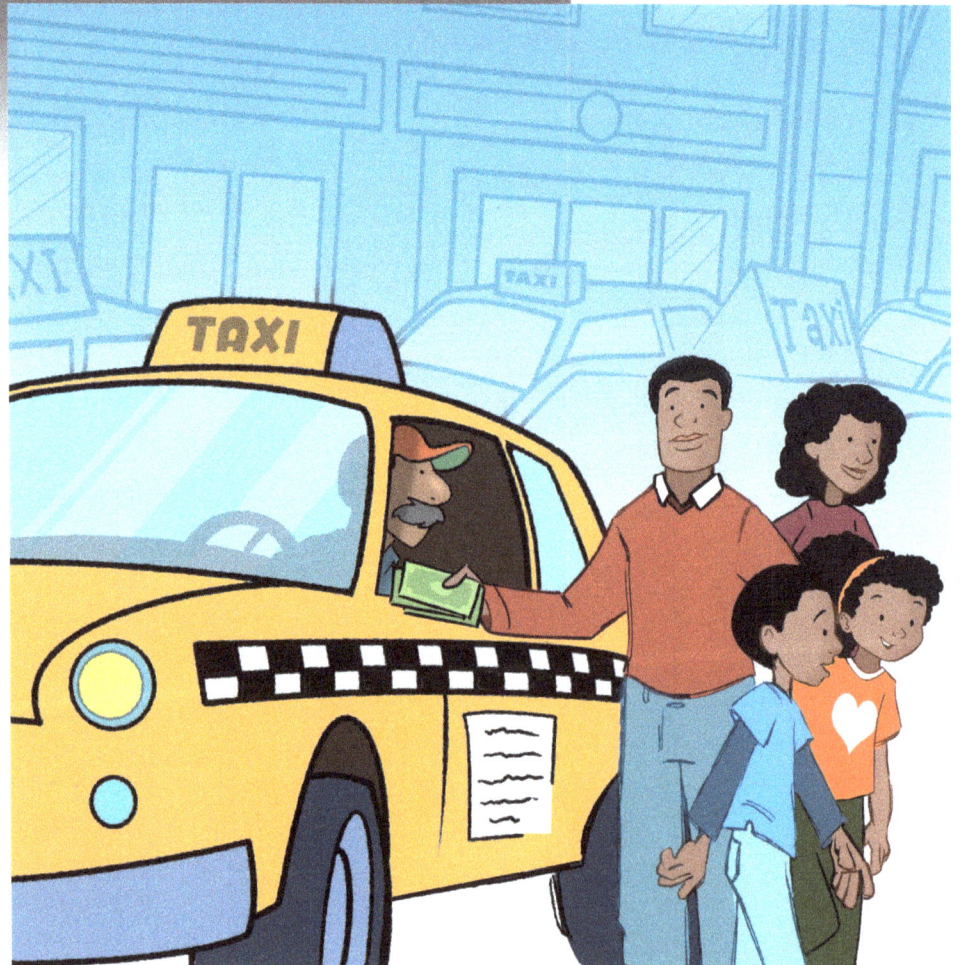

1. Lemonade Stand
2. Movie Theatre
3. Restaurant
4. Grocery Store
5. Clothing Store
6. Gas Station
7. Airport
8. Taxi
9. Hotel

As the list grew bigger and bigger, Anthony thought,
"Wow, money can grow in a lot of different ways!"

Suddenly, the school bell rang, and Anthony had to quickly go to his next class.

riiiiiinnnnnnggg

Anthony thanked his
teacher and waved
goodbye as he left
her classroom.

Ms. Wilson, with a big smile, thought, "One day, Anthony is going to be a very successful adult!"

Running down the hall to his next class, Anthony thought, "One day, I am going to own the things on my list and make my money grow!"

www.ingramcontent.com/pod-product-compliance
Lightning Source LLC
Chambersburg PA
CBHW060800150426
42813CB00058B/2770